LIFE

...for dogs and other people

An anthology

by

Deirdre Golden

Edited by Nigel Corlett

ISBN 978-1-4461-8892-7

First Edition 2010

© 2010 by Deirdre Golden

British Library Cataloguing in Publication Data.
A catalogue record for this book is available from the British Library.
First Edition, 2010. Published by Nigel Corlett in conjunction with www.LULU.com.

The poems in this anthology were previously published in the five booklets listed below, under Deidre Golden's pen name of P.D. Pemberton, and privately circulated.

LIFE-as it occurs
LIFE- slithering by
LIFE-here and there
Looking at LIFE
LIFE-in bits and pieces

Front cover illustration by Nigel Corlett
Drawings of dogs by Paul Golden
Booklet covers by J.P.Lavender and Paul Golden
Printed in TrebuchetMS 12 point
Technical Editing by Angela Allen: angelaallen06@hotmail.com

Published by www.LULU.com ID Number: 9201507

INTRODUCTION

These collected poems, (or pieces of verse as their author calls them), span several years. Deirdre Golden has written them as they have come into her mind. They show two aspects of Deirdre's life: her interest in words and her love and understanding of animals.

Deirdre, eleven years old when I first met her, was quite determined in her view that animals mattered as much as, if not more than, people. The school we attended in the1930's was run on very relaxed lines. Lessons took place in the mornings and games in the afternoons. All the staff had dogs, (could it have been a condition of appointment?), many of which accompanied them. The headmistress proceeded in her stately way followed by two King Charles spaniels.

One school holiday Deirdre went to work for a dog sanctuary. At the end of the month all dogs not claimed or adopted had to be put down. This proved agonising for Deirdre, who telephoned all her friends every time.

Since then, in spite of a very busy life, Deirdre has worked unstintingly for various animal rescue organisations, both in Britain and abroad. Many of the poems, as readers will realise, spring from her own experiences. I well recall the occasion when she found the starving pig.

I hope the readers will have as much pleasure as I have had from this collection.

Sheila Caink

CONTENTS

WORDS, WORDS

Words we utter in profusion
thus creating the illusion
that they're brought
about by thought.
Talking birds lack this confusion

ALACKS

They say with quite peculiar pride
they have no head for figures, no ear for music,
nor a head for heights, so must turn back.
But a sense of humour and imagination
are what no one claims to lack.

WILD LIFE

Without binoculars I cannot tell
a bison from a buffalo.
All I know
is that our butcher offers bison
but not buffalo.

It seems the latter travels faster
and the butcher was too slow?

REMORSE

"I'm sorry that I bit your hand", the patient said
"-an action that I now deplore -
but my wife's turned vegetarian
and I'm a hungry carnivore."

LOOKING BACK

You'd think that Looking Back
-what older people do -
would be a static occupation.
A time of reminiscence or review,
a time of contemplation.

But sometimes there's a need for speed
-if it's looking back to find
a bustling London bus
or a brisk rhinoceros
approaching from behind.

HAUNTING REFRAIN

Pray, what makes you think that,
while I bear-with-you,
I want to listen to
that relentless syrup music
with it's repetitive refrain
before you yield my bank balance
or the time of the next train?

SANG FROID

"Where have I been", she said
"-well, I got stuck in a lift all night,
when shouts would go unheeded,
But it was quite all right.
I had all that I needed.
I'd taken the Telegraph to read
and a torch to read by
and my sandwiches for lift travel...
And, came the dawn, I blew my hunting horn"

PASTURES NEW

A bassoon-player left the orchestra,
retired to the country for a rest.
But soon felt life had lost its zest.

He bought a rowing-boat, but found
bassoon-playing while afloat
was hard; and was apt to run aground.

He turned instead to nature conservation,
protecting flowers, butterflies and bees,
took up research and observation
of many creatures' lives,
including tracking insects and their wives.

When last seen
he had become quite keen
on following wood-lice to their destination.
-which goes to show that those who live with a bassoon
need have no fear of giving up too soon.

WHAT IS IT...?

An ostrich is a wondrous sight
as are sea-horses and seals.
What is it about men
that they stand and stare
at machinery on wheels?

NO HYDRA, HE

He put the dinner in the bath
and put the baby in the pan to stew.

A woman's like an octopus,
simultaneous.

What a man can do
is one thing at a time
not two.

YOUNG MAN . . . .

Young man, your new fiancée's very dear?
Before you settle on a wife
remember, she should last for life.
In an inflationary era
your loved one will become much dearer.
The state does not stand all repairs

-it's you who'll have to pay for spares.
If you were to buy a horse
you'd look into its mouth of course.
If it were a car
you'd estimate how long, how far.
In other words, you'd calculate
how soon it would depreciate.
Well, will she stay the course?

If she's sibilant and hissing
perhaps she has a few teeth missing.
Every time the dentist fills
you will have to foot the bills.

Never mind her violet eyes
and whether they are matching
unless to your surprise,
when rapturously near
she is rather apt to peer
and blink.
Then think:
will she very shortly squint?
New glasses could cost you a mint.
Never mind allure.
Will she easily insure? .. .
.. or shortly need re-thatching?
Does she tend to be rheumatic,
is she balding fast?
She may, like tyres, be pneumatic
but, like tyres, will she last?

PRESIDENTIAL WIFE

A Presidential wife
needs to be residential.
And also needs a steady nerve
with hair that won't rise up in public glare
and several central teeth to bare
in consolidating smile
that doesn't swerve

A Presidential wife
needs
white gloves to shake the hands that come in single file
two eyes that gleam
and do not seem
to be looking down
her nose-for-doom;
a leg or two to show in times of national gloom,
a good stomach for news and foreign food,
a twenty-four hour laugh that's never crude,
strong hands to massage Presidential brow. . .
. . . and must know how to place her feet
(not in her mouth, which must be too petite).

A Presidential wife
has one helluva life.

HOLDING ON

Ne quittez pas
-Don't go away -
the French succinctly say.

Here, it's no longer "Hold the line"
but "Bear with me"
-as though they think you'll marry them
for ever and a day.

THE CATCH

O Daughter Mine, surrounded by an aura
of lavender cologne and/or a
hint? a pint? of Miss Dior
which precedes you through the door -

marry a fishmonger if you wish.
There ought to be a future, monging fish.
Even vegetarians have cats
who need supplies of plaice and dace and sprats.
But when the wind is in the west
you'll never need to guess
what time your loved one will be home
with bits for bouillabaisse.
And if you wake, with dreams of bream pervading the night
air,
bouquet of prawn at dawn will prove your loved one is still
there.

If you don't want to hint of halibut
O Daughter Mine, you'd best stay celibate.

A SCOT

When watching pundits on tv
there is a tendency
to believe one who's a Scot.
His speech, guttural and abrasive,
sounds emphatic, seriously dogmatic,
not subtly English, ambivalent, evasive.

His lack of elasticity
seems like authenticity.
He, surely, will not lie?
-this man from mountain mists and rain-filled lochs

who can look you in the eye
while wearing woolly skirt and woolly knee-length socks.

POLY<u>WHAT</u>?

One pair of hands is not enough
for all you have to do?

Give polyandry a try.
One to wash and one to dry.

FACE TO FACE

Time was, when <u>privately</u>, a kiss
beneath the apple tree was bliss.

But nowadays kissing is routine
daily on the tv screen.
Singers, foreign diplomats, dribbling soccer players all do
this.
Quiz masters, show biz personalities embellish their
banalities
with kisses for a total stranger who is someone else's Mrs.

Let us all give several cheers
for judges, all-in wrestlers and Peers
who manage to restrain
themselves; and (currently) refrain.

Small wonder, when so many kisses now abound,
there are international germs around.

PROXIMITY

You would suppose
they'd move their toes
out of harm's way
when right behind you in the queue,
not stand so near
to peer and overhear
what it is you do and say,
breathing their germs into your ear.
Like muddled sheep they meld and weld
with you
as though they have to be
in absolute proximity.

What can you do?
Well, you could try a
cry of "FIRE!"

CULTURE BY COACH

By all means coach off to Abroad
cosily compressed
with the 41-strong eager horde
of cultural voyeurs, off to be impressed,
all glistening while listening
to Mr. Wilderbaum from Illinois
who seems to feel the need to shout
his joy at seeing places he has read about.

Queue for coffee, queue for loo,
back in the coach by twenty-two.
Pack and repack crumpled clothes,
prepare some exclamations
for the guide's next explanations.

Tour museums with this earnest band,
trip to watch fish being canned
and stand and stand
waiting for Mrs. Benjamin
who <u>found</u> a loo; but got locked in.

Watch <u>others</u> row at sunset on the lake
(during your twenty-minute break).
Listen for but do not hear
the nightingale, since Mr. Wilderbaum is near.

Sample the delights
of so many designated Sights
And listen to their history.

How kind! But no, no thank you, not for me.

NOT LESS (UNLESS)

If your wife went on a diet, you'd be inclined to say
"I've got less wife than before."

But a Mormon whose latest wife had run away
would be obliged to say
"I now have fewer wives, I'm sad to say"
unless, improbably, the rest of them had all got caught
in a revolving door
and left slices of their bodies on the floor
so, arriving at the airport where they'd weigh
his luggage, he would want to say
he had less wives than yesterday.

THE CANDIDATE

How to select, whom to elect?
Give me a politician
seeking my support
who's capable of thought.

But never mind the content,
start with topography
as demonstrated on TV.

A smile which shows his teeth, but not obsessively,
should show him affable, but not excessively.
A lisp, hint of a squint, disarming stutter
(concealing what he fears to utter)
may render him appealing.
(Too much to hope he's wise?)

But, for me,
he'll jeopardise
his chances if I see
the whites of both his eyes.

FROM ABOVE

On a heat wave summer evening, still and clear and blue,
you think that you would love
to float serenely and poetically among birds flying by
to view life from above
-to view life in perspective,
cool and calm, reflective
in silence of the sky.

Your mentor huffs and puffs, inflating the balloon.
The basket's small, the burner's hissing hot,
the giant fire extinguisher does not leave a lot
of space. Your mentor suddenly climbs out.
"You won't go far", he says,
(by now he has to shout)
' -the air is running out."

The crowd below looks upwardly in awe.
There are not any birds about.
They'd gone up to their nest to rest
shortly before
you join them slowly and majestically
in their overhanging tree.

"THOUGHT IS FREE." -William Shakespeare

Computers, clever devils, can communicate,
co-ordinate
and calculate
and analyse
and summarise
and synthesise
and memorise . . . . .

but they're not like me and Shakespeare,
wise.

LATE STARTER

Impecunious Herbert left it late to take up larceny.
At the jeweller's for a watch repair
he saw a glinting diamond
part-hidden by the carpet there.
If he were discreet and shuffled with his feet . . .
He bent quite casually to retrieve
it, put it up his sleeve . . .
but, I fear he'd left it late to start this new career.
As he leaned and bent I am afraid
he dropped his glasses, teeth and hearing-aid.

NORWAY AND NEW ZEALAND

Norway and New Zealand have lots of sea and scenery,
coastline and attractive views.
New Zealand offers free
hot water from its geysers
and Norway, for a breakfast dish,
several kinds of cold and beneficial fish.

But I expect they wish
their countries also had
some news.

DAISY

If, short of cash, you feel the urge
to kidnap, first do your research.
Daisy's kidnappers did not do this.
That's why their kidnap went amiss.

Daisy said she'd not be missed,
-her mother's memory was hazy
-father'd gone to be a monk at thirty-three,
left them an ansaphone for company
-but her mother was profoundly lazy
and when home alone
didn't listen to the phone,
-so wouldn't know what they had said
about returning Daisy dead.

From lonely tower in the woods
the kidnappers had quite a way
to go to ring with their request
-and hear nothing.
They had little rest.
They had to walk as well to bring
cheese sandwiches for D.
three times a day during her stay.
As they were three,
at least they had a four for bridge at night
in a fluttering candlelight.
All that walking through the wood
helped keep them fit; but did their bank balance no good.
The ringleader, with aching feet and spirits low,
said "Let me be quite frank -
we'd best send her for sandwiches and go
and rob a bank."

RECOUNT

At lunchtime, on the news, we hear the reader say
of a government Minister
' -away on holiday today,
he swam in a heavy sea so rough that he may
have been carried far away."

Agog, we listen in at night
and realise what he means
isn't "may" but "might".

OVERHEARD AT DOG AGILITY

"Thanks for your note of sympathy . . . .
but Auntie's had a good innings, was over seventy three,
and we all know
it's just the way she'd have wanted to go -
a day of excitement and suspense.

If only she'd survived to see
Rex get his rosette for Agility -
-it was Auntie who fell at the fence."

LOBSTACLES

There's always something to be grateful for.
You're not obliged to be shouting your wares down on the
quay,
"Fresh fish, fresh fish"
constantly

-or, if you've broken two front teeth,
'Freth feeth, freth feeth".

And when you're invited to a "do"
people, sniffing, do not back away from you.

THE BISHOP'S BLUES

A Cambridge Blue in younger days,
the bishop hadn't been agile for quite a while
when he went for the night to the deanery.
He decided to have a bath while the dean's wife got the
tea.
'twas a pity that he didn't see
the dean's wife's Wet Paint sign.
Once in the bath, he gave a shout
"I'm stuck. I simply can't get out!"

Leaving the bishop in the lurch,
the dean rushed off to deputise at church.
The dean's wife stayed at home to bishop-sit
-in case the house caught fire -,
produced conversation through the bathroom door.
She didn't tire . . .
The bishop, growing colder, older, searched his mind for
something to be grateful for.

"I rather think", he said, "that I should like a drink."
The dean's wife, disappointingly, came back with a cup of tea.
"As you won't be down for dinner, I've brought a sandwich and mince pies." she said,
discreetly covering her eyes.
He couldn't turn around
to reach. She couldn't see.
The food dropped in the water,
where it drowned.

The dean, returning, told his wife
"It was you, my dear, who
chose the colour royal blue . . .
Tomorrow I can ring the chemist. He'll know what to do."
"By then the bishop will be blue
with cold" his wife anxiously opined.
She paused for thought.
"Still, I'm a monarchist,
and he'll be royal blue from behind."

DEAR, DEAR

In their sad loss, the French lady
could not think what to send.

So sent a card "In Memory
Of My Expensive English Friend."

AT EIGHTY

Grandmother knits as she drives.
("I can't sit here static,
this Jag's automatic")
-so that, by the time she arrives
even without traffic blocks
she's produced several socks.

The traffic police, horrified,
panted up and waved to the side.
"Pullover, madam, pull over!" they cried.
"No, no. It's just socks", she replied,
"- the needles would be much too wide,
when you're moving at eighty and it changes to top
while rounding a bend, the stitches all drop.
I know this because I have tried."

The police brought out hankies and cried.

FLIGHT

The customer with rolling eyes rushed in the bank. "No, no,"
she said, "Tell Mr Pettigrew
it's not a question of cash-flow.
It's simply that cash flew."

ON ICE

They show no flicker of dismay when facing Eastern food.
It seems they are not rude
enough to hiccup, yawn or have a mighty sneeze.
Not a nanny- but a hypnotist- must have taught the Royals
to freeze.

COUNTRYSIDE

It's the fault of English literature
as well as rain -again
that what we mean by countryside
is a soothing English scene
in soothing English green . . .
. . . and not Siberian steppes
or swamps of everglades
or where grey camels stand
on monotonous grey sand.

I shouldn't think that scorpions
relax in crowded cities.
I suppose that they suppose
where they reside
is countryside.

ACCESSORIES

Why should it be
that reading glasses, man-made teeth can cost a mini-bomb
but hearing-aids can come quite free?
Could it be
that the government wants all to hear
what it bellows in your ear?

ROMEO AND JULIET

At that crucial time
had Romeo and Juliet
but been carrying mobile phones . . .

.. their pathos
would surely have been bathos.

WAIT BEFORE YOU PERAMBULATE

If you must perambulate
then, Madam, kindly meditate.
If you don't want your latest young to bear the prefix Late
-then wait.

Have you ever heard of a protective parent bird
-or a mother platypus -
who wouldn't hesitate
but would precipitate
its enprambulated infant straight
in front of a determined bus?
Madam, either recede
or else precede your new-born, pram-borne heir
-or wait
instead
until the buses have gone home to bed.

UNCLE HERMIONE

My Late Uncle Hermione
had a twin sister called Humphrey,
since at their christening
the vicar wasn't listening.

DUO

They've pedestrianised the market-place
so, from afar,
in fact, from here,
we can all hear
the butcher and his wife,
who leave their door ajar
while learning trumpet and guitar.
They're big and strong and have the strength
but lack the ear.

GOING, GOING . . . .

One of life's simple pleasures
is studying the physiognomy
of one losing their punt pole
with surprise.
No need for words, no need to surmise
their thought. It's all there in their eyes
in stages one to three
rapidly.
One: "Ooh, I'm slipping off the boat!"
Two: Disbelief, emphatically,
"It can't be happening to me!"
Then three: "It can! It is! I'm going down
-and shall I drown?"
as they disappear
dramatically.

LOST FOR WORDS

At this point in time
at the end of the day
without these clichés
or the word infrastructure
what should we all say?

A SADNESS

Last week, I met a Japanese
who seemed to be about to sneeze
and had a blink throughout the day.
I rather think
he had something to say.

LEPIDOPTERY

Their son-in-law was a lepidopterist.
(They found him in a dictionary).
He went lepidoptering along the cliffs . . . .
and was found face down in the sea.

Her father told her
"If you can, for your next man
find one not so energetic,
one less peripatetic
like a docile tax inspector or
a Funeral Director."

LOOKING AHEAD

They were a cautious couple, looking well ahead.
"Look before you leap" was what they always said.
They read weather forecasts, horoscopes,
share prices, racing tips,
took binoculars and sandwiches with them on their trips.

When they swam out side by side they looked ahead
for boats and rocks; and watched out for the tide.

What they failed to do
was see the crocodile behind
with jaws that were open wide
enough for two.

CHRISTMAS HOSTESS

At Christmas time, the cooking wife
revealed none of her turkey strife.
Despite the many mouths around
she uttered no unchristian sound.

The beast seethed all the palpitating while
that she, with hospitalitating smile,
dispensed charm and sherry to both Age and Youth
remaining gracious, calm, serene and couth.

At oven door, whence nothing could be heard,
she spake her mind unto the raw and bloody bird.

COMPOSURE

When you retire and can relax
you are supposed
to be composed.
-and so you are -

of artefacts.

FORMER PEOPLE

They were all people a long time ago
then they became personnel.
Now they're re-named Human Resources
will they soon be re-cycled as well?

HINTS FOR THOSE NEW TO DRIVING

WER WUMP! WER WUMP! Bump -bump -an unusual sound?
A mechanic should be found.
Mind you, if he's competent, he'll find
that cauliflower bouncing on the seat behind.

When you're parking on a slope
to pop into a shop,
if the handbrake isn't tight
your lovely car'll take off in flight,
pointing down the hill.
It's inadvisable to grab the bumper
to make the beast stand still.

When you return to your parked brand-new car to see
a biretta or three triplets on your upholstery,
get out fast and scout about.
When you've managed to locate
your own, memorise your number plate
-unless, of course, the bonnet
has pink rabbits painted on it.

Wanting to reverse when it's very dark
in the multi-storey car park,
get out with the torch before
you go. Now count your wheels.
(There should be four.)

Intrepid you, in France, and now
-you don't know how -
you've come to be facing three-lane traffic at the lights,
all pointing towards you
Those eager, throbbing French drivers are waiting for the
Go.
You do not know what you should do.
Keep calm. Keep still.
Let those eager, throbbing French drivers
avoid you...if only they will

OR

Or

is a simple, unassuming word
that, with imagination, could be used much more.
That man prone in Harrods' store
looks the worse for drink, you think,

Or

he may be hunting wood-worm in the floor
or hiding from his mother-in-law

Or

a muslim, thrown by British Summer Time,
who's stopped just there for prayer

Or

a man without a safety pin whose trousers have begun to
tear
he's just heard an eager customer for sale-price shirts shout
"four"

Or

he's just dropped dead on Harrods' floor
when sales are going splendidly
so no one's free
to scoop him up and out through a back door.

REMEMBRANCE OF THINGS PAST

I've given up remembering
my mind is used for thought instead
-there's only so much room inside my head.
Information can be stored elsewhere
-if only I remembered where.

SPECTATOR

In other times biography was written to be read.
Its subject often was quite safely dead.
But now his life is spread out on tv
(quite possibly erroneously)
for all, including him, to see,
as though he were not here to hear.

Programme producers peel back layers of his life,
shred his personality.
Insensitive, intrusive, impertinent, impenitent,
they explain to us and him
what he'd meant by what he'd said,
analyse his motives, foibles, taste in ties and wives .. .

If a celebrity, he will, like us, prefer instead
to pay visits to tombstones
and read there what is said
of those who are quite safely dead.

NO SPELUNKER

When you are cursing with your mashie niblick in a bunker,
Rejoice that you are no spelunker.

A spelunker is a man or woman or hermaphrodite
who goes down deep, where there is no light.

THE LONDON STARE

If you're parochial or provincial, used to bus stops, cars and air,
what upsets you most in London is the Stare.
In the evening, homeward bound, the zombies of the underground,
hunched and bunched before their time below the ground
will just sit there and stare -
their bodies here, their spirits where?

You never see a moving eye glance briefly for the evening sky.
Have they sub-human feeling as they rumble out to Ealing?
Provincials wonder with misgiving if they're living . . .
They stare through you with those Weimaraner eyes
that do not seem to recognise or actually to see a thing.

If only, in the underground, there were a few more wasps around
to sting.

TRAFFIC POLLUTION SOLUTION

If you held tightly to a kangaroo
and were quite sprightly too,
you could go hopping
off in unison and just a few
enormous leaps to do your shopping.
Lashed together, you could bound and bound about
that delaying roundabout
without stopping.
When you'd got your shopping
you could stock it
in that useful and capacious pocket.
. . On the other hand,
it would be grander to meander on a camel to the bank
and park it in a camel rank.
if it were knocked down
by traffic in the town,
you'd need only an agile vet and monster crane
to get it on its feet again.

ON LOVE -A TRILOGY -

Sitting on the park bench in thick fog
he felt her warm and furry
-and found it was the dog.

The night was icy, crystal clear.
They were sitting on the park bench.
He never touched the wench.
She felt deceived; and found it queer.
It was all right.
So cold the night
his arm had frozen to the bench.

Sitting in the gardens on the seat
side by side, their feet
were deep in snow,
their hearts and eyes aglow.
Fluttering snowflakes fell while he
recited poetry,
melting her heart but not the snow.
They gazed into each other's eyes . . . .
. . . next day, a passing child with puzzled frown
called out in surprise
"those frozen snowmen on the bench
are sitting down."

HOMECOMING

Returning to the house that one has left behind
there are several things one wouldn't wish to find.
The worst things to come home to?
The remnants of a burglary -
a blocked-up loo -
or, a dying cockatoo -
or a note that said:
"Your dinner isn't in the oven.
I've taken it to my witches' coven."

HAZARDS

Last week I saw a country sign
which offered Free Range Eggs.
Just another hazard in the country -
all those eggs on legs?

THE ANSWER

When I win the lottery
I shall choose the right location
and call a hurried convocation
from near and far
of all the ansaphones there are,
put them in communication,
let them exchange their useless information.
The right location?
A beach where tides are high.
Goodbye.

HUSH HUSH

"Seul le silence est grand"
De Vigny opined.

Silence is golden. In modem life
there's all too little about.

So keep this in mind
and please do not shout
when those policemen kneel on your wife.

A FLUTTER

And if in stout and middle-age
you feel like prancing
at Greek dancing,
wish to flutter like a butterfly
on Wednesdays at the village hall,
you'll need a short and flimsy dress and
no sense of the ludicrous at all.

OLD- FASHIONED REMEDY

Advancing science had left Mrs Hepplewhite behind.
"You'd think, with all this modem technology,
with closed circuit tv
so the burglar at your door can easily be seen
on a television screen," she said,
"-they could invent a switch that would unhitch
your portcullis
and drop it on his head."

EXPORT

It would be difficult to find many
Mc Tavishes in Abergavenny.

The Welsh go in for export more.
Mutton, rarebit, male voice choirs or
fluent conversation.
With their peregrination
and miscegenation
they permeate the English nation.

EUPHORIA IN EMPORIA

They do not seem to need an art gallery
for aesthetic pleasure
but regularly use their leisure
in a modem Superstore, to spend their day
meandering, gazing glazed and in a trance
at the colours on display
of prawns and carrots, melons in array . . . .

getting in our way.

ELEGANCE

Elegance does not come naturally to those
who wipe their ice cream cone against their nose.

AH, RHETORIC

Observe how many men there are
in public life who cannot roll an r
and yet will express their views
through the media.
If cerebral, they could choose to be
an architect or an actuary,
not politician or academic
practising r-less polemic.

It's as though they cannot rest
until they've put their ws to the test.
And with the r that will not roll
they choose to talk about their wole

I have never met
a sad wheel-tapper yet
-or plumber or gas fitter who
had this affliction of the diction too.

Perhaps, to be realistic,
it's just a question of statistic.
So many, down the years, have come,
alas, to plumb
and gas-fitters and re-fitters come and go;
but I don't know

a wheel-tapper, unless
that man wearing the florid, floribundal tie
who gave his views on cowwect dwess
to wear at a weception
was not a lecturer in anthropology
but a wheel-tapper in disguise
telling lies.
If so, I owe lecturers in anthropology
 an apology.

APPEARANCES

"Always look your best" was what her mother said,
"and never look your worst".

So, on the beach in summer she was always seen well-
dressed.
She didn't look her best in her body,
which was seemingly about to burst.

AURORA

If this very morn
you saw the glory and the splendour of the dawn,
before it's time for tea
you'll be feeling ninety-three.

CAUTION

"Not without due care, officer,"
we heard the Irishman complain.
"I saw the lorry coming straight at me
so I took my hand down from the wheel
to cross myself, you see."

COME BACK CHEKHOV

At least your people moaned and pined
in words we understood;
and spoke of Life in epigrams.

They didn't chat in analogue and digital
and kilowatts and kilograms.

CHERISH WINTER

Cherish winter while it's here
with fog and frost and rain.
Because when spring comes round again you know what it
will bring....
the garden ants,
the kitchen slugs,
mosquitoes biting in the night
and wasps that sting.

CLING TO NATURE

So many scents and sounds and sights,
Nature's various delights,
still come quite free.

But dentists don't come naturally.
They charge a fee.

CONTOURS

If you're a doctor married to an architect
you can ask her to define
both heave and subsidence,
so you can diagnose your aging patients
with more confidence.

CONTRAST

Women, when they gather, talk of serious things,
like shoes and twins and curtain rails
and the cost of feeding husbands
-or how to capture one.

Men are much more fun.

CRABBED AGE

Carry me back to the days of Yore
when the nursery had a green baize door
where the cacophonous little dears
were splitting only Nanny's ears.

Modem parents I deplore,
Their offspring screech for more and more.
In the supermarket there's too much progeny.
I shall vote for more misogyny.

THE DAYS AHEAD

If you retire at sixty-five
And aim to stay alive to ninety-five
you'll have ten thousand nine hundred and fifty days
of wishin'
you didn't have to go into the kitchen.

A POSSIBILITY

Those earnest lady walkers
walking earnestly
in thick socks and unbecoming shorts
may well be having lovely thoughts.

PRACTICAL

When asked about their latest fiancé,
"Well, he's no oil-painting, no troubadour,
but very practical", they say.
(Like that multi-purpose bottle-can-and-jar-opener
they've got at £12-60 in the ironmongery store?)

DAY BY THE SEA

They parked judiciously
well up the quay
keeping at bay the salt sea spray.
With windows up against the ruffling breeze
they sat and glistened in their sanctuary.

The car roof, as a canopy,
protected them from shining, swirling, whirling gulls
protected them from unaccustomed sounds,
the tinkling masts, the plopping oars, the pinching winch,
the clash of sea on harbour wall, the flapping, slapping
sails,
the shingle's crunch,
the bark of happy, splashing dogs,
the distant cries of estuary birds,
the gently rattling reeds .. .

Untanned by sun or wind
unscathed by sand or tang of sea
unsullied by sea-weed
nor dazzled by the crimson-sinking sun on rippling waves

they had their sandwiches. And set off home for bed
hygienic as their packaged bread.

DIAGONAL

For winter warmth, save on electricity,
have a long dog on your bed.

But she'll turn out to be
diagonal.
(And two dogs are octagonal.)

THE DUCHESS

For her birthday treat, the duchess knew
what she wished to do.
She tried her hand
at sand -
yachting; and found she needed two.

-was mistaken for an ostrich in the sand
and
posted to a zoo.

DON'T DO IT YOURSELF

From a vantage point, such as this branch of the apple tree,
you'll find that tossing down gratuitous advice to others
comes quite easily.

ENGAGING LADY

She is engaging in every sense,
greets all she meets with charm and smiles
and brings delight.
And knows how to engage your attention
when it's time for Bonio at night.

ENTERTAINMENT

The TV programme for tonight
is one you can forget.
While it's on I rather think
you'll play Russian roulette.

ELEANORA CUMBERBATCH

Eleanora Cumberbatch
never won a tennis match.
Not that she lacked skill -
she had the eye, she had the speed
to move in quickly for a kill.
She simply lacked the will
to believe she could achieve
Wimbledon and fame
with the name
Eleanora Cumberbatch.

She ended up eventually working in the B.B.C.

FAST

O lucky us, today's housewives,
convenience foods to simplify our lives
can be cooked with ease.

They're jacketed and packeted,
we only need to heat.
We'd have quick meals to eat
if only we could open these.

FLAUBERT

Flaubert, a perfectionist, would polish just one sentence for
an hour.

Perhaps he did not stop to pop out to a shop
for a chop or cauliflower.

FIRST AT LAST

At last, at last,
I'd backed a horse who'd not be last,
who wouldn't pause to look for mushrooms on the course,
who could go fast ... . . .

Through field glasses I watched my horse
as it hurried round the course.
The first time it came thudding by
My hopes were high.
This was no outsider.

First past the post, it was alone
i.e., without its rider.

FLINGING

Have a fling or two -or three -
while you are young.

Herrick put it more poetically
and perhaps prophetically,
what is your youth if it's not flung?

But do not fling yourself too far
and end up in disaster.
It's not easy to be dissolute
with both your legs in plaster.

FORESIGHT

You read the horoscopes,
consult palm-readers
and the weather-forecasters.
Far-seeing and foreseeing,
you like to look ahead. . . .

I cannot read your palm from here
but, with the benefit of E.S.P.,
I can tell you where you'll be
by the end of this new century --

--dead.

A COLLECTOR

You can sludge through muddy woods to gather bluebells
or trudge along the shore amassing shells ...
but nowadays you can simply sit for a collation
of new words
such as annuitisation

HAZARDS OF THE ENGLISH LANGUAGE

The large lady from Iceland found
that her command of English wasn't good.
When, in church, they told her that she should
kneel on a hassock, she misunderstood
and knelt heavily upon a cassock,
which did its occupant no good.

GOING UP?

Alternative Arts

Fluent in English, you're articulate.
So language shouldn't bring you anguish.
Hispanic studies might just do
for your umbrella while you cogitate
how best to widen your horizons, (why you came),
en route to gaining fame.

Intelligent as well?
You won't spend student days
scrubbing burned saucepans at the sink.

Just think:
You'll have another fifty years for this,
scrubbing your way through married bliss.

Preservation, Conservation is the mood of late.
Do what you can
to help preserve that nearly -neolithic man
the dilettante undergraduate.

Play Hamlet, (Juliet for a change
-to show your range).
Play hockey, chess, the saxophone,
play politics, with public speaking.
Get known.
Join Guild societies, frivolities and jollities.
Reintroduce the art of streaking.

Do not roam
to lectures. The Union's your spiritual home.
Consult your dictionary. Restore
gay to the meaning that it had before.
If in Finals your emaciate Spanish
seems to vanish, try
some Latin to get by.

Put up for president, to gain an extra year
(in which you'll wine and dine)
to prepare for life Out There.

OUGH!

Imagine you're a foreigner, full of anguish
in efforts to pronounce the English language.

You thought it ought to be
like thaw when there is no t ...
but no, it's though like no,
not thou like Slough

-which isn't stuff like rough,
which isn't just like cough or off.
Yet through is just like threw;
and a borough's not a burrow
but like thorough.

Those who can get through these with ease
need not resort to learning Japanese.

QUITE

Quite so.
-which means that you agree my statement that
enlightening
a foreigner about the use of the English word QUITE
is quite difficult (rather difficult).
Some would say it's quite impossible (totally).
"It's quite cold outside" (fairly cold).
"The bath water's quite cold" (very).
"The orchestra's playing was quite brilliant" (superb).
'He's quite clever with figures" says the modest parent.
(Read "very")
"Henry's quite hopeless at cooking" (completely)
'Scooping scones into a paper bag at a royal garden party
isn't quite the thing" (not at all the thing)

"She looked quite elegant" (very. Element of surprise)
"The groom's quite forty" (at least forty)
'His morning suit doesn't quite fit" (doesn't fit)
"Quite, quite" (Yes, yes, but don't be indiscreet)
"But he's quite sober"(not at all tiddly)
"I can't quite see what she sees in him" (I can't see it at all)
"Have you quite finished your diatribe? (shut up)
"Our magnolia / the rat / Uncle Fred was quite dead"
(irreversibly)

That's quite enough.

HIGH NOON

Before high noon my thinking's minimal
in fact, totally subliminal.

Why else would I
hang my cup of coffee up to dry?

ISLAND LIFE

She said to the solicitor
"Now we are the only two on this deserted isle,
there must be something more
that we can do to while away the day.
Daily date-picking is such a bore."
She went up close and looked into
his only eye.

Stepping back, he said in reply
'I might try to get some driftwood,
then we surely could
draw lines across the sand and
make a crossword by and by.
That would make time fly."

Envoi:
Don't get shipwrecked with a lawyer.
He'd be sure to bore yer.

JANUARY HURRAH

In January the sea is grey.
The beach is windswept, biting, bare,
hurrah. All those others are not there.

KERNOW

When the wolf-pack of reporters want to know
where the Minister intends to go
for his holiday,
he can quite confidently say
Kernow -
sure that they won't know the way.
Even a Cornishman may wonder if he ought
to have Kernovian on his passport.

LATER ON

Dine late.
(Who wants a nursery tea
just because they're seventy-three?)
Get up late to compensate.
Put on sailing trousers
and hurry to begin
lessons in hang-gliding
before death can set in.

LADY LEONORE

Iconoclastic Lady Leonore did not feel
a European; but British to the core.
When she met and married Helmut Glockenspiel
she felt British even more.

LONG LIFE

It seems a woman ages faster
than a man; but is a longer-laster.

which may explain why, in the supermarket car park,
there is one elderly man guiding you back into that
tight space against the fence while there are eleven
elderly women plodding their shopping along in front
of your car bumpers.

METRICAL MADRIGAL

Come centimetre with me along the slippery lane
to see the buttercups, observe that plane
up there at 600 metres
on its route of countless kilometres.
Down to the lake, dark with many thousand litres
beyond hectares of land
and stand
to pick blackberries by the hectogram or so
through mud coining by demi-kilo.

When we climb down from the stile
we shan't plod home a weary mile
but eleven hundred metres.

PHONE DWELLER

That compressed, condensed lady
who dwells inside our telephone
and says in calm and dulcet tone
that our alarm call's cancelled now
makes us wonder how
she knows so rapidly.
Don't you agree that she must be
one of the wonders of this century?

REMINDER

That chirruping you hear in the early morn
isn't sparrows in the attic celebrating dawn.
It isn't birds at all.

It's your fire alarm high, high up in the hall
telling you its battery has nearly gone.
Unless you feed it with another
it will go cheeping on and on
and on
and on
and on

RETIREMENT

A normal man, retiring with a well-earned sigh,
hopes to get a fishing fly
or lie
watching the birds wheel in the sky
-or see the sailing boats sail by
-or stand and watch his beans grow high . . .

He doesn't want a rag to ply 200 tins of Chemico until he
die .. .
Oh no.

No more do I.

THE QUICK (AND THE DEAD)

I once knew a gravedigger
who dug in a heat wave
only to find, when lunchtime came,
he'd dug out the wrong grave.
The vicar there slowed down the hymns
and elongated each Amen
while quickening, molten gravedigger
dug, dug and dug again.
The coffin's owner lay in state
as he was now both Late and late
for the first time in his life
(well, death, to be precise).
He now had cause to pause,
metaphorically on ice.
Though late this first time ever,
it seemed a time for Better Wait Than Never.

Those with self-congratulatory smile
who say they've waited "such a while"
have no call to be unctuous
because they're always punctuous
they may not be compunctuous.

There was the drama critic
who <u>would</u> arrive far, far
too early for the bar
and well before the play.
His punctuality knew no bounds,
he wouldn't brook delay
on humanitarian grounds.
On the night his visitor was left locked in the loo
his wife, in the excitement, lost a shoe.
Now, oddly shod, she had to limp and hop
and, like a kangaroo, arrive by bounds.

It really isn't couth.... to be on time if lacking ruth.

R.I.P.

Elberfeld and Eisenhower
were hamsters of E registration.
The As to Ds had gone before -

-hamsters are of short duration.
The cat, after meditation,
realised it was carnivorous,
could not resist temptation.

May Elberfeld and Eisenhower rest in puss.

PIOUS HOPE

Your young son's <u>not</u> innocuous
and his sister is cacophonous.
So when you're out on Sunday
please do not load them ophonous.

RIPOSTE

"Urgh! I couldn't work in that muddle!" they say
with supercilious eye,

"Well, we all have limitations"
is the right reply.

TO RUPERT

You say Dad's lying face-down on the ground,
his head among the flower pots?
Ah, he must have accidentally found
your skate-board, left lying around.

SHARE

Share your life with someone who
can grasp the humour of the situation
when those burning omelettes
cause a conflagration.

TALL STORY

Columbine and Celestine were twins and six feet tall.
In their cottage bedrooms they stretched from wall to wall.
Their heads brought plaster off the ceiling in the hall.

-and when they tried to milk the goats, they had to crawl.
Their father pondered this; and ultimately said:
"You overdid it, Agnes, you had more daughter
than you oughter.

As we can't sell the twins, we'd better sell the goats
 and breed ostriches instead."

SHORE IN SILENCE

There comes this fantasy,
summer by the sea
seen as a silent film
aesthetically.

Serene as swans,
mothers, in lilac toning with the sea
of iridescent peacock blue,
and fathers, wearing crisp white shorts,
in ballet strew
petals at the water's edge
in pas de deux.

The children gravely stand
in mildly undulating sea
with water to the chin; no cause
for anxiety
unless they open jaws.

No sound at all
in this summer of Goodwill to All

SPEECH SPEECH

A compulsive talker's someone who
is never heard
to utter a word
when two hundred and ninety seven will do.

SOUND ALL AROUND

Our poor cat takes fright
when hearing that Northern Ireland politician on tv.
Does he go on at that pitch day and night
through toast and marmalade and cups of tea?

THINKING POSITIVELY

She's ert and doesn't lack list
and <u>he'd</u> have less bale and dole and wist
if he had a more
trepid and defatigable mother-in-law.

THOSE PHOTOGRAPHS

When they invite you in and offer to display
their family in photographs,
that's the moment for dismay.
What can you say?
Mere photographs don't tell you much about the nature of
the beasts unless
they're wearing kilts or wooden legs or Red Indian head-
dress.
Yes, Yes,
at the wedding there's a happy groom
but even he's
having hiccups or about to sneeze.

Get your bid in first and say how very much you wish
they'd show you their collection of goldfish.

THOUGHT FOR THE YEAR

At least there's no ambiguity
in total vacuity.

TO THE POWER[N]

When you're on a tropic beach, away on holiday,
with a leg in plaster
while others have gone off to swim, left you all alone,
that's when you'll miss the opportunity
to play the numbers game on your home phone
where you could while away the day
pressing buttons one to three -or infinity -
with your insurance or gas company.

SEEING RED

At dusk, he locked her in the greenhouse for the night.
Quite unintentionally, a mistake that any man might make.

She couldn't break the glass as it was plastic.
Her patience not being elastic,
she ate all the grapes within her range
then, for a change began to smash
tomatoes at the plastic, in a tantrum.
Tomorrow's window-cleaner, though a man,
might just notice this new splash
of colour -should he come.

He later went to fetch tomatoes in
to put with bacon in the oven tin. He found his wife,
tomato-red.
With venom, she went to her bed.

"I'll have to have fried bread instead", he said.

SEARCH

If you want them all to love you
don't ask those probing questions.
Search your dormant mind.
If you rummage there
who knows what you may find.

UNCOMMON SENSE

"Use your common sense" they say
idiotically.
If your sense is quite uncommon, not of the everyday,
and experience has not taught
unravelling machinery ...
or if someone brought
a present of a rhino,
how would you know
what it would need for lunch and tea?

UPROAR

Invited to the opera, he said "How very kind!
I do hope you won't mind
if I come in my dark glasses
and leave my hearing-aid behind.
I don't wear it any more
For uproar."

WEDDING INVITATION

"I haven't a thing to wear for the wedding",
she sighed.

"Well, let's hope", he replied,
they won't think it rude
if you go in the nude."

A WELCOME

In flowing floral housegown
she let him in.
"While my dinner burns,
tell me your troubles, do sit down.
How far have you come, how much do you earn?
And let me know your view of the morality of persuading
those
like me
to buy things that they do not need
with money that they do?
He was running late, he said.
He'd have to call again.
He left without saying when.
Her sister, in the kitchen, asked
"what was he selling?"
"He left so soon, no means of telling -"
She smirked.

' -but with hindsight, my extra-sensory perception
says he was a councillor campaigning for election."

WHAT AND WHY

What is the antithesis
of photosynthesis?
What questions are all the rage
but do not seriously engage
the mind, like why
don't clouds fall down from the sky?
We know what choice they made in that election
of a president -

but why, oh why?

WHO KNOWS, WHO KNOWS?

But use imagination,
leave prejudice behind.
Beneath that yellow baseball cap
there could well be
a mind.

WHY I BUY THE TICKET

And when I win the lottery
I'll rush out and buy a butler
who will answer the front door
saying 'Madam will be free at noon;
but not before. '

WITH A MORAL

The traffic warden put his head into her car
and spoke a paragraph or two.
"But I don't know what to do", she said
"I'm trapped by my seat belt. Can you help?"
The warden leaned into her car, tripped,
and fell across her lap. She gave a yelp.
A policeman with a fearsome frown
saw the warden's feet in levitation,
arrested him without hesitation.

The warden's learned now to be more discreet
when accosting strange women in the street.

HOLD-UP

When he set off for work that day
the hold-up gunman was depressed.
He'd completely lost his voice
so there was nothing he could say
to encourage the bank cashiers to pay.
The hospital was on his way.
There he saw a sign "Be a blood donor, give blood today."
He stopped and grabbed the notice, carried it away.
So, at the bank he held it with his gun for all to see -
And had a very profitable day.

WOOING

On a splendid summer evening
He wooed her on the river in a punt.
Melodiously, he sang the Eton boating song
as they floated so ecstatically along

. . until they had a shunt, a spill.
Unluckily for him
he found out retrospectively
that she couldn't swim.

SW3

In S.W. 3
you cannot easily look out to sea
to view infinity,
and eternity.

THE ALTERNATIVE

The pen is mightier than the sword they say.
If you haven't got your sword
(have come without it)
then you cannot cut your throat today.

Take a pen and write to tell them all about it.

A FEW WORDS

He asked, inquisitively,
"Where might your husband be?"

She answered "In the Swiss navy."
"Oh", he said, "I see."

ALL PLAY

If playing poker and the saxophone have begun to pall
there's a new game you can play throughout the day -
measuring various envelopes to see how much to pay.

THE CURE

She would visit him quite often
when he was trapped in gaol.
To cheer him up she'd sing, well, wail
snatches of Grand Opera and would yell
some noisy hymns as well.
He retreated to his cell.

He resolved that, when he'd served his time,
he'd give up his life of crime
and do no wrong
rather than risk being trapped
by matrimonial song.

DRAW BACK

Madam, as you overhang the kerb, waiting to cross
kindly hold your stomach in
or my car will get quite cross.

FELO DE SE

If you choose death not by hospital but sea
and are planning suicide
then avoid a flat beach with a fast-receding tide
unless you're very agile.
You may have to hobble ankle-deep
for half a mile.
This will take a while.

FEATHERED FRIENDS

Though young, he used to spend his time indoors.
Therefore his parents bought him a young hawk
so he could take it for a country walk
and go to the petshop for fricassée of day-old chicks,
its staple diet.

No. <u>You</u> wouldn't want to try it.

FODDER

Cars only stoke up on fuel
to give them strength to reach their destination;

but people think and talk
and buy and consume their fuel
as a full time occupation.

GETTING, GETTING, GOT

Getting On suggests progress,
success with what you want to do.
But it can mean, too,
that butchers, bishops, professors and Prime Ministers
are all younger now than you.

GERALD'S CURSE

On the course, when Gerald sliced his shot
and it went awry
'Donner und blitzen' was his cry.
Then he found an antibiotic
sounding suitably exotic.
So, if you're near the green and hear the call
'Flucloxacillin' you'll know that he
has slotted his opponent's ball.

GOOD NEWS

The broadsheet morning papers rightly inform us all
of international suffering and strife.
But the rural weekly papers
show another side of life.
Those brave young men abseiled down the cliff
to save a goat; and brought it up again,
The octogenarian sailor, on his boat,
is still afloat.
And assorted ladies, with their several smiles
are setting out to walk for miles
in aid of charity.
You'll see them near the happy, winning marrow on page
three.
If you want something positive,
a rural Weekly is where you should live.

A GOOD LISTENER

You have many problems -
Henry's just failed his exam.
Zoe's sipping whisky in her pram
and that blocked drain will have to wait
until Percy's home from gaol again.
You don't know what to do.
The world is lacking in Good Listeners -
go down to the zoo.
Take your troubles to an elephant,
-he won't go away
but will stand listening all day.
If you look into his eyes
you will see that he is wise.

HEREDITY, ALAS

Red hair and flat feet run in families, they say.
But it was not anatomy that came the way
of the Chiddingfolds, just disaster,

The daughters weren't adept with locks and keys,
could get locked in loos with ease.

Mr. C., solicitor, on his way to court
had crab salad for his lunch
and heard his man-made teeth go crunch.
At court, he couldn't thpeak to plead his case.
His client, the defendant, angry red in face,
threw a punch at Mr. Chiddingfold's crab lunch.

Though not a blood relation,
Mrs. C. had good cause for agitation.
Late for her plane and in a state of stress,
she slammed the car door locked, trapping her flowing
dress,
and in her distress dropped her car keys down a drain.
In order to get free again, she used her wits,
took scissors from her bag and cut her dress to bits.
She tottered, tattered, to a taxi
not to her plane for Spain.

LIFE

If life is something up with which
you haven't lately caught

pause and wrap yourself in a lovely thought.

LIFELESS

Those who stare at afternoon tv
must have homes quite bare
of lost passports, shoes and pet hamsters and such -
they can't be living much.

LETHAL

Gazing at the cricket ground,
ruefully he shook his head.

"Tom wuz our opening bat", he said.

"But two days ago 'is granny landed on 'is 'ead
and cracked 'is skull. 'E wuz extremely dead."

We wondered; malice aforethought?
Or merely manslaughter?, we thought.

He went on.
"If 'ed a looked up 'e'd a'seen
that 'is chimley pot 'ad begun to lean."

LOOKING AND LISTENING

You can hear and you can see
much that is macabre on tv,
most of it unintentionally.

NOT YET

His mind wakes up at eight each day,
eager for the fray.

It's just his body causing the delay.

PROTEST

Aunt Lilac doesn't want to sit with other elderlies
(who knit).
Now she can't ski, play squash or polo any more
or to deer-stalking on the moor,
with men is where she'd rather be.
She sets out with determination
for absolutely any Demonstration.
She does not discriminate, simply wants to Agitate,
so goes off to Protest with zest
where she'll find men by the score - no, men galore.
You'll see her on the tv news in plastic mac with a placard
on her back
liking to rant and chant and shout, waving her arms about
with great elation,
knowing that then she will aquire two men.
All to herself, she'll get two men who'll lead her
handcuffed to the station

PRIORITY

Londoners wouldn't know the etiquette
for narrow, winding Devon lanes
where a car reverses to the edge
of the hidden ditch with prickly hedge.
The other car gives a wave of thanks
as it skirts the overflowing banks.
The first car waves back in reply
to thank the thanks as it squeezes by.
A London driver in a car
doesn't know how civil we all are.

SPOTTED BY THE LEOPARD

The leopard I was chatting to the other day
said "Tell me pray,
what is it about Man?
While the rest of us dine on the hoof,
catch- as- catch- can,
he puts his food into a pan to heat
before he feels that he can eat."
It paused for thought -a thinking leopard, he-
"I suppose that it must be
so he can talk interminably
about the process on TV . . .
. . . and thus receive a fee."

SPECTATOR SPORT

In these days of the precocious limousine
we are denied the entertainment previously seen
of anxious, puffing ladies pushing their car up the slope
in the hope that what goes up will, in the end, descend.
And at night we are denied the sight
of men in evening dress, white tie and tails,
cringing there
with a starting handle in the evening air.

THE NUMBERS GAME

A university, planning a new hall of residence
with clusters of rooms for student groups,
wondered how many in each group would
relate and integrate.
They asked an anthropologist
who came up with the answer: Eight.
So, madam, surely two
sets of triplets would be enough for you?

and the number in a football crowd should be
one hundred and seventy three.

TRAVEL HINT

Whatever is the reason you want to leave the plane
- you got on the wrong one, and want to emigrate -
- you're due now down in Parliament to open a debate -
- you're expected at the Palace for a luncheon date -
- you want to get to London in time to catch the shops -
Don't be precipitate.
Don't get off the plane before
It stops.

MISSING PERSONS

Terrorists apparently give Switzerland a miss.
It seems they do not mind it.
Or, perhaps, they simply cannot find it?

TEA TOPIC

And can <u>you</u> see
the royal family
in its British way of life
over cups of tea
plotting how to take a life?

WALIAN

I met a Walian recently
who didn't know that he
was that sort of alien,
had to consult his dictionary.

WEIGHTY WORDS

This is a splendid - very heavy - dictionary.
three hundred thousand definitions is its claim.
With so many unknown words on every page
one hangs one's head in shame;
but if those three hundred thousand words were instead
heavily inside one's head
one would not be able
to raise it from the table.

YONDER

On yonder hill his cottage is in isolation
surrounded by silent vegetation.
No purring cat, no guinea-pig, no budgerigar,
no cow with whom to share the view,
no waiting mouths, nothing for him to do . . .
He must feel the need
for ducks or hens for him to feed.
He must lead a barren life
     –   unless, of course, you count his wife.

DIALOGUE

She lies on her back in the summer sun,
her legs up in the air
so that you may soothe her stomach while she's there.
She licks the stroking hand in appreciation
and we have this silent conversation.
Her message now lies wholly in her eyes.
"And now some Bonio would come in handy -
Yours hungrily, your loving Candy."

DOGS

Dogs, like rugger players and women Christmas shoppers,
are pack animals. They do not care to sit
in isolation like a cat, to spit.
What brings them elation is Good Conversation.
They like to lick your paw,
especially if it's offering more.

RAPPORT

The afternoon was very still.
The bullocks were all lying in a group.
We wondered what they were wondering
and if they were wondering what it was
that we were wondering too.
This takes a time
and needs someone with nothing else to do.

We went and breathed into the nearest nose.
In reply, it sighed and blew
and dribbled a bit too.

We'd got our message through.

It's sad that there are those who
have something else they'd rather do.

SERVING SUGGESTION

When you serve a soggy meal and it looks jaded
what you should do
is say "the fish fingers have all waned".
This being intransitive, it means they've done it quite unaided
so no blame will attach to you.

SANCTUARY

The donkeys graze or browse or drowse in summer sun, in
fields above the sea.
Retired or rescued spend this last lease of their life in
sanctuary and tranquillity.
On windy days the donkeys run to greet, their necks across
the gate.
Your troubles must be left behind.
Observant eyes and ears and eager noses wait,
They're urgent to communicate, insistent for your mind.

The timid ones, who have known harsher times, stand far,
Look longingly, view and review.
Their trust comes slowly as the summer air and must be
delicately earned.

If you are patient, wait, and wait, and wait.
As though testing ice upon the pool,
Nose tentative, eyes wide and questioning,
They come, and ultimately gently lean, to demonstrate that
there is trust in you.

In winter barn's pervasive donkey warmth
Is peace of mind; and, strangely, of spirit
From their innate ability
To bring you, in their sanctuary, tranquillity.

DEFINITIONS

But definitions go, you know.
One lost, which is sad,
is that of a cad.
It used to be a man who
gave her two halfpennies for the penny slot
in the ladies loo
--or one who hid his golf opponent's ball,
or who wanted to enthral ie: appal
by Telling All.
Now, those who set out to impress
by Telling All are rewarded by the Press.
. . . .
The professor's favourite definition
was that of Gentlemen.
"They are those who know
how to play the saxophone
and do not do so."
. . . .
A Diglot does not speak a lot.
Not being multiglot,
he reckons two will do.
. . . .
Age is when the milkman and the dustmen
no longer call you Madam
but address you now as 'Luv'
-but the traffic warden's more discreet.
(And, while we're on the subject,
ask about his rheumatism and his feet.
Few do.
So he'll willingly tell you . .
and Bill can sidle by and move the car well down the
street.)
....
A True Friend is he who knocks you over with affection
then after a short wait,
licks you to resuscitate.

A DEVON DEFINITION

Grockles are immigrants to Devon, non-maritime,
who settle on the coast to sniff sea-air
and then find that they have to share
it with the residents, i.e. the gulls,
and complain that these should not be there.

AN ASSET

Not computerised,
nor a digital product -whatever that may be -
but an asset of versatility
alarm system
healing agent
insect-repellent
deliverer of letters
a source of extra winter warmth
a means of mopping crumbs up off the floor
an alibi for journeys you don't want to take
this is also a morale-booster.

-Telepathic, patient, optimistic . . .

It is, of course, a dog.

ASCENT

They talk loosely of getting up
from bed
when they mean down instead,
not rising.

It's only when you've briefly slept on dog cushions
and floors
you find it not surprising
that dogs stay on all fours.

ASCENT (OLDER)

When you arise you realise at once
that rest
is what would suit you best.

BOUNDING

That beaming mortal, humming happily
as it bounds along the crowded street
must have a very clear conscience
-or shoes that fit its feet

BIRTHDAY

On this your latest birthday
you are feeling old,
in fact, dilapidate?
Never mind the date.
Cheer up, let it be said
that many of your age are already dead.

CAREERS SECTION

When you grow up and aim to be
a t.v. critic for that glossy, narcissistic magazine
you'll be blinking at a fluttering screen
watching programmes you will wish you hadn't seen.

CORRECTION

Dear Sirs,

I may have misinformed your company
in my recent letter about your man who came to install
our electric meter eight feet up the wall
with a dial no one could read.

> I apologise.
> I now realise

that an active lady gorilla could probably succeed.

DOUBLE TROUBLE

Who knows? You may soon
aquire a clone
so will no longer be alone.
But can you contemplate
living with you in duplicate?

CLAIRVOYANTS ??

Milkmen, anaesthetists and the clergy
have to rise before it's light.
Let us hope they have good sight.

CAN'T WIN

They complain when the heir apparent
reads their papers and gives his considered views
on current topics in the news.
Perhaps they would prefer a figurehead
with nothing bubbling in his head
sitting on the throne.
'No useful purpose' they would say
'-sitting simply
smiling limply. '

DISARM

If incompetence is what you do best
(then never aim for Everest)
set out to be disarming.
Simply practise being charming.

DELAY

Tired of her constant nagging,
he led her to the cliff to push her over
then saw protruding from her pocket
the key to his Range Rover.
So decided to delay
the treat for another day.

DIVERSIFY

If life is routine, dull and lacks diversity
snatch a trifle of adversity.
(Francis Bacon held the view
that adversity was good for you.)

Strapped to the coastguard, get winched up the cliff.
"Don't look down" they say.
But on this clear, bright day
you do, to get this splendid view
of sparkling sea and all the bay
beneath your feet
300 feet down, down below.

What they should have said, though,
was "Don't look up" -to see
as you ascend, a few feet from your nose,
the crumbling chalk and tumbling scree.

Or, in the club for international students,
get locked in a loo.
What you must not do
is shout for help; but display British phlegm.
Put a note down on the floor beneath the door
"Help. I can't get out".

When the workmen finish their lunch hour
and take the hinges off the door
you will be welcomed, as you emerge,
with a roar
from foreigners come to applaud
Something they've not seen before.

Or, walking dogs with a wrist in plaster
in the muddy fields, lose a lace from your left shoe.
All you need to do
is lace it up again.
So shuffle home in all that rain.

Or, nearer home, get a urine sample for the vet
from your evasive bitch.
Pursue her with a dish with which
to catch the liquid -if you're quick enough
to crash beneath the fruit bushes, prickly and rough
to get there in a minute
or your dish will have nothing in it.

Or, as did a friend, you could go
to Sweden in its winter snow
to teach English every night.
Hers was an unusual plight.
On her first morning, when her landlords were in town,
she popped out for her letters in her flimsy dressing gown

so light to pack for travelling by air
but not too suitable to wear in all the snow out there.
She left the door ajar, quite unaware
that it would close on her.
As she didn't care to stand out in the Swedish ice and snow
she was obliged to go
to a neighbouring house, to shelter there
speaking no Swedish, shivering, she just stood.
The neighbouring wife soon understood
she should take her to her kitchen
before hypothermia set in.
"The most exhausting part -"
she later said
'-was mastering the art, (in dressing gown),
for three hours of showing appreciation
by facial expression
with no words for conversation."

FASTER FOOD

You, like some of us, may not like
setting out to hunt for food
(for which you have to pay.)
Be glad, though, that you do not have to gallop
after it when it runs away.
And be glad that you're not someone else's prey.

FOOD FOR THOUGHT/ THOUGHT FOR FOOD

"You are what you eat"
they bleat.
And will repeat
"You are what you eat"

Let's forget the food and drink.
You are what you think.

HEALTH

Health is useful for the body
You will find,
but you'll find it a boring subject
for the mind.

AN INTRODUCTION

Now they're on their way in their historic Daimler
on their first visit to you
you've discovered you're co-habiting with a mouse or two
what can you do?
Meet them head-on
saying they must doubtless miss
wild life in the metropolis
so while they're here it will be nice
for them to meet your mice.

IN LINE

As you're not in the Marines
and don't have to stand in line
you need not queue like vertical sardines
with your feet on mine.

KINDRED SPIRITS

If Noel Coward and Winston Churchill were back here again
they'd be out there with umbrellas
puffing in the rain.

LOST

What happened to as though?
It's like no one wants to know.

LOST SKILLS

Do not mourn the faculties you have lost
count instead those that remain.
The topmost apples on the tree you can forget.
Applaud yourself that you still retain
the A.A.'s phone number in your brain
for that puncture in the pouring rain
so they, not you, will get so very wet.

A MODEST HURRAH.

Hurrah,
theres a splendid clock inside my car
but which is its switch?
in autumn it stays ahead
a mathematician can easily calculate
the time, not to be late
and gets practised in deducting the extra hour

It's in spring when the head is used to the deduction
those with an appointment
are liable to disappointment.

MISSING

On the radio we hear that inflation's growing quicker
than we thought
and the government's improving things slower than it ought
and so on.

We know hedgehogs are diminishing;
but where have all the adverbs gone?

MERELY OBSERVE

Next time you switch on the tv
turn off the sound and simply see
the better to discern
the technique of actors and the odd M.P.

You will be spared that soprano with such energy
that if she doesn't stop
she'll burst that expensive evening top.

NO OPTION

My seat-belt with vice-like restraint
will not let me be
sitting comfortably.
But then, Her Majesty
similarly,
is subject to constraint
doomed to sit high above the audience
where opera uproar rises loud and clear
much too near her ear.

NOT ALONE

It's odd that one so small and non-aggressive as a mouse
can bring such turmoil to a house.
You buy a humane trap to lace
with cheese. Put it in place.
Before going to your bed, so much to do.
Pick up every crumb you've left in sight,
hide the dog's bone in the oven for the night,
hang up the fruit in case the mouse is catholic in its taste
and doesn't like your food to go to waste,
move newspaper and plastic bags
so it can't chew them into rags
to make a bed in which to rest by day.

When it's caught, you'll take the trap to a garden far away
for release;
but how to choose
whose?
At midnight, place the trap where the dogs intrusive nose
cannot get
caught. But -disturbing thought-
is it a rat, perhaps -
too big for both the traps?
And do all those recent nibblings
mean it has brought siblings?

Don't wait.
Simply emigrate.

DO NOT COME

If you will insist on staying non-computerised
you mustn't be surprised
if you become a landmark in the village
and achieve a certain fame
day-trips will come to view you
our quiet village will never be the same.

ON THE WATER

You'd think it patently unwise
to go up the estuary with three dogs on board
an old dinghy with a kick-start outboard
able to tangle in that scenery and greenery
where the swans have settled down to rest
in their new-built nest
there are other places one can seek-
But there are optimists up every creek.

ON THE MOVE

Well! Good gracious!
After twenty years you're moving to a house that's spacious
(You'll need several nooks and crannies
if you take grandpas and grannies.)

Upheaval is the term; but you
up in the loft will find there's heaving down to do.
When you move in, you'll find the bath's the spot
Where the removal men have dropped a lot

-the cat's basket, the fishing rods, the fishing bait,
your left wellington in mourning for its mate
but mercifully not the pianola and the garden roller
They're out there in the rain.
P'raps the removal men will come back again?

Search for a major perquisite,
the water stop-cock. Where is it?
Don't take your gas cooker,
use electricity instead.
The gas oven would be tempting to your head.

PROPOSAL

She said, when she rejected his proposal yet again,
"I don't complain that you don't speak Swahili
and try to play the oboe now and then
it's simply that you're colour blind" she said
"and always drive through traffic lights on red."

SEEDLESS

Those who are lucky and can read
the small print on packets
need not feed
on such quantities of bird seed.

SURVIVAL

In middle age they are discreet,
gaze demurely at their feet
when others probe to know their years
particularly if they're hers.
But when they creak, after 60 or so
they're glad for everyone to know and crow
that they're 78
and not yet Late.

PEOPLE

So many individuals are really quite delightful.
So many in the multitude are entirely frightful.

THERE'S ALWAYS SOMETHING

Now Fidel Castro's gone
and Mister Al Fayed may perhaps pause for breath
we can concentrate on other worries,
such as water-voles' decreasing population
and how a toad can cross the road without annihilation.

THINGS COULD BE WORSE

When you're cursing as you go rushing
through the day
realise you'd have more cause to cuss
if you were a 3-legged octopus.
Life could be much wuss.

THIN MAN

That thin, dilapidated man
who shows such signs of stress
has an energetic wife
with lots of P.A.S.

(P.A.S.: Power Assisted Steering)

UP AND AWAY

You've always longed to learn to ski?
So had we. So seized an opportunity.
Friends back from the French Alps, where they'd learned
with ease,
offered to provide their skis
and took us on a moonlit, frosty night to a narrow ridge
in the Malvern Hills, where we sat on icy, scintillating snow,
feeling superior to those below,
as we struggled with the straps to fix
the skis into a place
where they could meet our feet. Prodding the ski sticks
is an art when your feet are well apart
on the icy track.
Still sitting on your back
you try to rise -in vain.
You're soon down on your back again.
For half an hour you're up and down
well-warmed by this unusual exercise
until, quite suddenly, to your surprise
you're up and off and gathering speed
sliding on ice towards the precipice.
What you now need
is news of how to stop before the drop.

The friends are up above, behind.
You call to them "Please would you mind
telling us how to stop?"
They shout back, most earnestly "You don't learn how to
turn, to stop
until Lesson Two".

TOPIC FOR THE DAY

When you are a genuine antique
and can be heard to creak,
you'll find the body rules the mind.
With teeth and shoes that do not fit, you will forget
not only where you left your glasses
but all about Tibet,
the Middle East, and what the world's leaders
should now do.

Your topic for today, most boringly, is you.

VIEWPOINT

"There are eleven things to do first today"
she said, as was her way.
"You haven't got to do the lot" was his reply
' -you won't be a wicked sinner
if we just have sandwiches for dinner.
While the sun is in the sky
come swim with me.
"What is this life, if full of care?"
come savour life while it's still there."

TELEVISION

Television nowadays seems ingrown, narcissistic
so many things it offers to the eye
are ephemera; but, to be realistic,
so are you and I.

ANNA'S MISSION

The morning he had strained his back, so didn't rise
but lay upon his bed
she went wagging up, then registered dismay.
She ignored the other dogs, went up to lick him thro' the
day.
When summoned for her evening meal
she stayed upstairs to lick, to heal.

DISMAY

The large and very fat, determined bee
was clambering furiously but unsuccessfully, in vain,
to rise vertically between stiff cardboard and the window
pane.
I had to scoop it from the narrow space
with an envelope in order to by-pass
the dog's all-too-eager mouth
and soak the creature in a glass.
I dropped it down the kitchen drain.
It fought back, came squelching up again.

After half an hour, I'd won the day.
The running kitchen tap washed it away.

Three hours later, I went into the kitchen and saw,
amazingly,
a thinner-looking,sopping bee
with spindly legs struggling, striving to rise up from the
drain
so had to dash its hopes and body into water yet again.

I'd never thought that I should be
so dismayed by murdering a bee.

HOPE

When we came upon her there,
abandoned, lone in a field of mud,
she did not stir,
lying in her squalor and despair.
"They give up hope, you know"
said summoned vet.

We took her water from the stream.
Slowly, she struggled to her feet
and drank copiously, alarmingly.
"Pigs drink like this from hunger"
said the vet with quiet anger.

When we returned with food
she came to meet, snuffling to greet.
She'd rediscovered hope.

SILENT PACT

In his high-chair he behaved beautifully
ate all his lunch up dutifully
but found the stringy cabbage hard to chew
He worked out what to do.

Smoothly, surreptitiously,
he passed it to the dog waiting so discreetly down below.
An unspoken agreement
that others must not know.

POST SCRIPT

The government may have left the voters in the lurch
but the Bishop of Exeter turned up at the station
offering rail travellers free chocolates
and inviting them to church.

NAMELY

If you need something to be grateful for,
look in your phone book,
Where you'll see...
Mrs. Squirrels, Mrs Haddock and Mrs Merrilee.

GROWTH

As they grow much older
some vital words elude their grasp,
leave them in the lurch.
So, while they're standing there
to search, they talk and talk irrelevantly
to fill the empty air.

JAWS

Somerville and Ross said the Irish put their fun
before their food.

Conversely, modern Britons
perversely put food into their thoughts and words,
describe catering more and more.
They're not afraid to bore.

QUANTITY

What is it about a multitude
That robs it of its pulchritude?

FRUSTRATION

In the bathroom, the Vice-Chancellor
was rapidly rehearsing his annual address.
When he dropped and broke his man-made teeth.
Loud was his distress.

SYMPATHY

When I gave a mighty sneeze
the dog jumped down from her bed,
came and sat, looking up earnestly.
"Are you all right?" she said.

ALL EARS

I used to visit donkeys almost every day
They like someone to talk to them.
Topics can vary, cricket scores to poetry,
They do not discriminate.
If you rub their noses and expatiate
They will wait, and wait, and wait.

THE ART OF CONVERSATION

Those of fifty plus , when they've finished their commuting,
All rush to learn computing.
And I.T.
-think it will come quite easily
to an experienced brain-
go off to evening classes, keen to learn
-but not, alas, retain
and have to start again.

Word processors now fill their homes, their lives, their minds,
Need all their concentration.
Their spirits eager but their knowledge meagre
They lose the art of conversation.

On the phone you hear their stress-
They agitate in great distress
When their machine's perverse.
They curse but don't converse.
They hardly hear a word *you* say,
Cricket, weather, other topics gone,
They ramble on and on
about their life of strife.

KEEPING IN TOUCH

If, while you watch the news
You let your glasses co-habit your ear
with your hearing aid,
You'll find your grasp of world affairs
Is not entirely clear.

England now seems thoroughly demotic
so some aim to be despotic.

BIRD LIKE

She has the bright eyes of an eager, searching bird
she talks and talks
like parrot and alarmed pea-hen
tall, she walks like emu or a cautious hen.
She doesn't need to fly
as she's not pursued by men.

MORE WORDS

I'd like to be more voluble in rhyme
but now my bank has sent 54 pages of tightly-packed
helpful, 'important information'
I may not have the time.

CAPRICIOUS

At the June election the morning paper said
the government had withdrawn its proposal to award
each citizen who went to vote
a free doughnut as reward.

COMMENT

Crossing the Place de La Concorde
she leaped for safety on a traffic island.
The leap wrenched off her skirt hooks
so the skirt waved polymorphic in the traffic.
The observant French policeman
ignored a passing car
and observed, "Là là!"

EXCHANGES

The nation may lack money in its till
But has treasure, in its language, still.
Aeons of correspondents' conversations,
Written confabulations,
have kept it alive.
With exchange of allusions, illusions and conclusions,
Convictions, contradictions and predictions,
Descriptions, speculation and illumination,
-words for preservation-
have helped it survive.

Now that mobile phones and textphones can be heard
Replacing the written word
With messages like yep and nope
Has the English language any hope?

PRECISION

Nowadays, precision in the spoken word
is not always heard. Does not seem to rate.

Precision now is for the digit
pressing those beastly buttons
in Remotes and mobile phones
and hearing-aids which screech and don't abate.

WONDER

To travel is to free the mind,
to leave its well-worn grooves behind
as, rising swiftly from Heathrow,
you leave bank manager
down
down
down
down
below.

Those who are wistful in a train,
Haunted by the wheels' refrain
-Never again, never again, never-
when on horseback or on skis, elated by created breeze,
gasp joyously at Ever ......Ever. ..
welcome infinity, eternity.

Infinity, eternity
are there for anyone to see
up in the sky.
Do you in tensely-knotted tie
pause to consider as you fly?

HABITAT

I never met an admiral in Leamington tho' there could well
be a Rear one there. Admirals, like lobsters and sand flies,
seem to settle in the salt sea air.

COLOUR CONSCIOUS

If your floors all have black carpets
and your sight is growing dim
you'd better have a pale blue dog
so you won't tread on him.

TACIT

Suppose you had arthritis in four legs
but lacked the words to grumble or to bore -
you'd simply have to sit
tacit on the floor.

SKILLS

I'm not adept at Grand Opera
nor moving hinges off a door;
but can say 'Help, Help' in Italian
since there's many a slip
'twixt deck and shore.

FROM THE DOG

Those people over there
have no sense or scent
of who has been near.
Badger, several rabbits and roe deer.
All they know is what they at this moment see -
No sense of history.

NO, NOT A NEW MOON

-a new boon in television.
Sub-titling bobbing up the screen
showing what you have this instant seen
and heard.
Sounds of a word it can enscript
but sometimes not the meaning too.
In a dialogue, a questioner may ask
in transcript
"Well, wooden Jew?"

TIMES PAST

It's tempting nowadays to reflect on Times Past
when cars and gas cookers and marriages were meant to
last.

LOSSES

You've lost your wallet and your winning lottery ticket down
a drain
so you'll not see them again?
Well, spare some sympathy for a landlocked lobster
who's suffering loss of memory, so doesn't know
which way to go
or a Naval captain expecting a royal visit
who unwisely had a sticky cake
and lost his two front teeth in it.

IN PINK

The woman magistrate had overslept
and was running late
so fetched her morning papers from the garden gate
in her pink -striped dressing gown.
A passing felon of the town
stopped to blink.
Then gave her a wink.
Some weeks later, when he had sinned,
they met in court.
She was looking down with a magisterial frown.
Then he thought of the pink dressing-gown
so simply winked and grinned.
She thought this contempt of court,
that she ought to send him down.
The moral, you may well think
is do not go out for your Times
in a dressing gown that's pink.

TIMING

I don't suppose that Beethoven had two boiled eggs and
then said
"I shan't answer the front door,
I shall compose a symphony until nearly half past four."

Similarly, verse writes itself at inconvenient times
juggling with rhymes now and then
up the fields or in the bath
when there is no pen about
and the fish is singeing in the oven,
waiting to be let out.

ENVY

In your need for speed
you wish that you had two back legs.
But realise that those
are for reaching food bags with your nose.

GOOD CONVERSATION

For Christmas what I should like is an alpaca
or three or four
or more.
They're genial, it's said.
I could flee the turkey that is dead behind the kitchen door
and go
up to their field for a word or so.
But -if there were floods or deep Christmas snow
they would have no grass, alas
so I should have to go
without Good Conversation and instead
carry their several Christmas lunches
to them in their shed.

TO CUSTOMERS, SPLENDID SHOP

That splendid shop has a sign outside
"Well-brought-up dogs are welcome here inside.
But kindly tie your children to the goat-posts we provide."

END IN SIGHT

If you live in the South West by the sea
you have opportunities urban dwellers are denied -
fresh sea air and lovely scenery.
And can go on steep and quickly -crumbling cliffs
and swim in fierce, engulfing tide.

OPEN HERE

O bring back those brown paper bags
Our teeth, not being elastic,
can't gnaw through all that plastic.

OPINION

When our heat-wave came
for two whole days
the dog took the view
that Noel Coward's mad dogs and Englishmen
was all too true.

AFFIRMATIVE

Yes is a word sub titles do not
seem to choose to use
we shall yet doubtless see
both a bishop and a judge
with a yeah which slips from their lips.

WATER

Water does not run uphill, they say.
Let us put them right.
If one night,
you wear your husband's pyjama coat,
when you go to the basin
your sleeve, spacious and capacious, long and dangling,
will engulf the flowing tap
and without delay
the rushing, gushing water
will rise all the way.

M.A.J.S.

(for an old friend)

We don't see her so often now
but picture her at dawn
out in the field with her O.B.E.
in wellingtons and nightdress
feeding her horses every morn,
a shivering hive of industry.

EN ROUTE

The path to hell
for those with several sins
is now composed of innumerable and assorted rubbish bins.

DIVERSIFY

Now times are hard, hairdressers find
fewer clients coming near
they'd better listen carefully
to make blackmail their new career.

VOCABULARY

Her voice precedes her body through the door
and then goes on for more and more.
For their next lodger they'll have shubunkin,
picturesque and never heard to utter a word.

NEW NEWS

If, tired of politics and warming globe, you
need something new to worry you
well, swine fever is pandemic now say scientists
and, don't forget,
they're mentioning that the planet Mars is due
to crash into us and obliterate the world.

(But not just yet.)

FIN

Those who retire and can live a life of ease
take up bee-keeping or pottery or Portuguese.
I shall learn the harp, instead
to be ready when I'm dead.

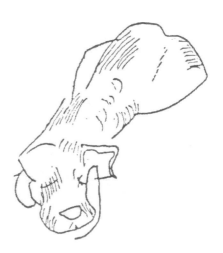

A - Z List of Poems

111

First Line Index

115